Sandy's Picture Stories

Sandra Price-Hosie

www.trafford.com
North America & international
toll-free: 1 888 232 4444 (USA & Canada)
fax: 812 355 4082

This book features original lessons for beginner adult English language learners. The materials are designed for an interactive cooperative multilevel ESL class of adults.

Each unit features:

- Eight randomized illustration cards
- Eight randomized key word cards
- Eight randomized sentence cards
- Correct sequence of sentences
- Scrambled words
- Scrambled sentences
- A listening cloze
- The complete story
- Comprehension and discussion questions

The topics of the units are drawn from current needs and interests of adult newcomers to North America. They are designed to augment and enrich existing curricula for beginner adult ESL students.

All the units are designed to be copied by teachers in full or in part for use in the classroom. All the units are the sole property of the author, and copying for any other purpose requires permission from the author (e-mail: price-hosie@shaw.ca).

The materials are designed to be printed by any regular printer onto pastel-colored light card stock to be cut up into colored sets of eight cards. Usually, light card stock comes in packages of five colors: pink, green, blue, yellow, and white (avoid using dark colors). Alternatively, and for more than five sets, copies may be printed on white card and outlined with a highlighter pen using a different color for each additional set.

For one unit, the teacher may make eight pictures, plus either eight key word cards and/or eight sentence cards. All the cards are numbered out of sequence to challenge the students. The section of the unit "Reading and Listening" contains the correct sequence of sentences for silent and oral reading practice, plus scrambled words for vocabulary retention and scrambled sentences to review vocabulary and syntax. The paragraph contains the same story sequence but uses advanced vocabulary and grammar followed by comprehension questions and a listening cloze exercise.

Lesson Suggestions

Copy card square pages onto light colored card stock. Then cut into cards, making colored sets of pictures, key words, and sentences.

Engage the students at the start of the lesson by silently acting out the story, eliciting ideas and vocabulary words or sentences. When students can't get it at all, show a picture clue and make sounds while you are acting.

Distribute the picture cards to pairs of students. Have them sequence the cards to "make a story." Using the "whole-class write" method, have students tell you the story. Edit into better English as you print the sentences on the board. Teach/practice oral reading, and then have the students copy the story and read it to their partners.

Distribute the picture cards to pairs of students. See if they can "make a story." Then distribute key word cards and have students match them and refine their story. Teach pronunciation and have students practice saying the words while pointing to the correct picture. Have students copy the words.

Play a memory game with the picture and word cards turning all over and mixing to start, and then turn over first one and then a second to try to get pairs. When a match is made, the student keeps the pair. When a match is not made, the cards are turned over again for the next player.

Distribute sentence cards with the picture cards and have the students match the cards. Check for correct sequence. Mix them and have the students change partners and repeat the matching exercise. Then turn picture cards over to remove visual clues and mix sentences. Have the students sequence sentences then turn over picture cards and match. Practice oral reading. Change partners for more reading practice.

Have all the students do the scrambled words and scrambled sentences. For more advanced students, move on to the final activities in each unit for oral reading, comprehension questions, and listening activities.

Use the final unit for creative writing, listening, and speaking. Distribute blank forms to students singly or in small groups according to their levels. Working individually or in small groups, have them make their own story board, key words, and sentences and then write their story and share it.

Contents

UNIT 1: Starting the Car (Picture Story)

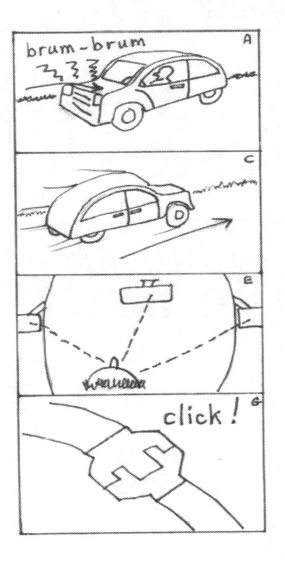

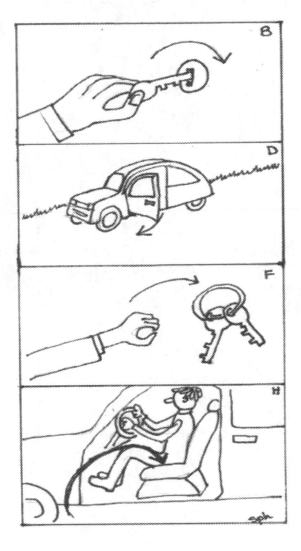

UNIT 1: Starting the Car (Key Words)

Sit	Get
Drive	Start
Buckle	Check
Open	Put

UNIT 1: Starting the Car (Sentences)

Sit behind the wheel.

Get the car keys.

Drive away.

Start the engine.

Buckle up.

Check the mirrors.

Open the door.

Put the key in the ignition.

UNIT 1: Starting the Car (Reading and Listening)

1. Get the car keys.
2. Open the door.
3. Sit behind the wheel.
4. Buckle up!
5. Put the key in the ignition.
6. Start the engine.
7. Check the mirrors.
8. Drive away.

Scrambled Words

1. road orc
2. smirde iror
3. pluke cub
4. part sut
5. genein
6. inotinig
7. lehew
8. enilosag

Scrambled Sentences

1. car the away drive.
2. ignition key put the the in.
3. engine the start.
4. wheel behind the sit.
5. the open door car.
6. belt your seat up buckle.
7. the mirrors all check.
8. car the get keys.

Starting the Car

First, you get the car keys. Then you open the car door and sit behind the steering wheel. Then you buckle up your seat belt and put the key in the ignition to start the engine. Now you check to see how much gas you have. Next, you check your side mirrors and your rear view mirror. Finally, you drive away.

Questions:

1. What makes a car go?
2. Why do you buckle up your seat belt?
3. Why do you check all your mirrors?
4. Can you name all the "wheels" of a car?
5. What do you need to drive in addition to a car and car keys?

Listening Cloze: Nouns

First, you get the car _____. Then you open the car _____ and sit behind the steering _____. Then you buckle up your seat _____ and put the _____ in the _____ to start the _____. Now you check to see how much _____ you have. Next, you check your side _____ and your rear view _____. Finally, you drive away.

Listening Cloze: Imperative Verbs

First, get the car keys. Then open the car door and sit behind the steering wheel. Then buckle up your seat belt and put the key in the ignition to start the engine. Now check to see how much gas you have. Next, check your side mirrors and your rear view mirror. Finally, drive away.

First, you _____ the car keys. Then you _____ the car door and _____ behind the steering wheel. Then you _____ up your seat belt and _____ the key in the ignition to start the engine. Now you _____ to see how much gas you have. Next, you _____ your side mirrors and your rear view mirror. Finally, you _____ away.

Extra Activity

There are many types of transportation in addition to the car. How many can you name or draw? Make a list. Which type of transportation do you use? Which type have you never used?

UNIT 2: Getting Gas (Picture Story)

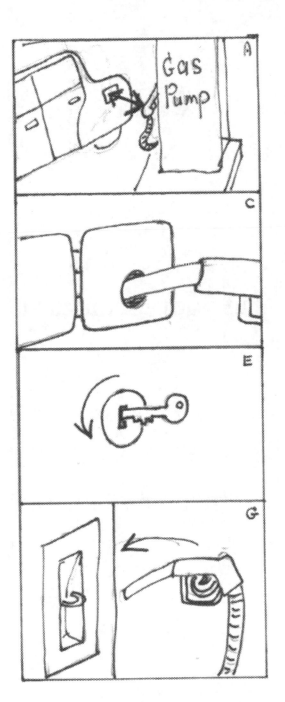

Unit 2: Getting Gas (Key words)

Keep pumping	Press the trigger
Park your car	Put your credit card
Put the nozzle	Return and replace
Turn off	Choose

UNIT 2: Getting Gas (Sentences)

Keep pumping gas until
it stops when it is full.

Put the nozzle into the gas tank.

Press the trigger to
pump the gas.

Park your car beside the
self-service gas pump.

Return and replace the nozzle
and take your receipt.

Put your credit card
into the machine.

Turn off your engine and
open your gas tank.

Choose the price of gas you want.

UNIT 2: Getting Gas (Reading and Listening)

1. Park your car beside the gas pump.
2. Turn off your engine and open your gas tank.
3. Put your credit card into the machine.
4. Choose the price of gas you want.
5. Put the gas nozzle into the gas tank.
6. Press the trigger to pump the gas.
7. Keep pumping gas until it stops when it is full.
8. Return and replace the nozzle and take your receipt.

Scrambled Words

1. pup samg
2. drat circed
3. gertrig
4. santagk
5. karp
6. lezzon
7. tripeec
8. runter

Scrambled Sentences

1. put the gas tank into the nozzle.
2. keep it full until it stops pumping is when.
3. return your receipt and nozzle the replace and take.
4. press the gas to trigger the pump.
5. into your credit card put the machine.
6. machine the credit put into your card.
7. open the engine and turn off your gas tank.
8. the gas you choose of want price.

Getting Gas

First, park your car with its gas tank opening near the self-service gas pump. Then stop the engine and open the gas tank. If you or anyone in your car is smoking, put out the cigarette. Get the nozzle from the pump and choose one of the three types of gas: cheapest, more expensive, most expensive. Put the nozzle into your gas tank and press the trigger to start the gas flowing. The gas will stop automatically when the tank is full. Put the lid back on your tank. Put the nozzle back, and if you pressed "yes" for receipt, take your receipt. Get back in your car, buckle up, start up, and drive away.

Questions:

1. What is the difference between self-help and full service?
2. Why can't you smoke a cigarette while gassing up?
3. What is the long form of the word "gas"?
4. What's the difference between economy and premium gas?
5. Why is the price of gas different at different stations?
6. How does a car make air pollution?
7. What is gasoline made from?
8. Where does oil come from?
9. What else can a car run on beside gas?
10. What is a hybrid car?

Listening Cloze: Verbs

First, _____ your car with its gas tank opening near the self-service gas pump. Then _____ the engine and _____ the gas tank. If you or anyone in your car _____ _____, _____ _____ the cigarette. _____ the nozzle from the pump and _____ one of the three types of gas: cheapest, more expensive, most expensive. _____ the nozzle into your gas tank and _____ the trigger to _____ the gas flowing. The gas _____ _____ automatically when the tank _____ full. _____ the lid back on your tank. _____ the nozzle back and, if you pressed "yes" for receipt, _____ your receipt. _____ back in your car, _____ up, _____ up, and _____ away.

UNIT 3: Stopped by the Police (Picture Story)

UNIT 3: Stopped by the Police (Key Words)

Siren	Where . . . ? Have . . . ?
Show me	Okay
Drive home	Problem?
Home	Here

UNIT 3: Stopped by the Police (Sentences)

What's the problem, Officer?

I hear a siren
behind me.
I pull over
to the curb.

Okay, sorry
to trouble you.
You can drive on now.

Where are you going? Have
you been drinking?

Here they are, Officer.

I drive home safely.

I'm just
going home, sir.

Show me your driver's license
and registration, please.

UNIT 3: Stopped by the Police (Reading and Listening)

1. I hear a siren behind me, so I pull over.
2. I say, "What's the problem, Officer?"
3. He says, "Show me your driver's license and your registration, please."
4. I say, "Here you are," and give them to him.
5. He asks, "Where are you going? Have you been drinking?"
6. I say, "I'm going home, sir. I haven't had anything to drink."
7. He says, "Okay, sorry to trouble you. Drive safely."
8. I'm happy and drive home safely.

Scrambled Words

1. niser
2. reciffo
3. selnice
4. loverlup

5. revird
6. lorbpme
7. kingrind
8. ecilop

Scrambled Sentences

1. you to trouble sorry.
2. home I drive safely.
3. siren the curb I over hear I to a pull and.
4. me your license show driver's.
5. the officer problem what's.
6. I here to him say are you.
7. drinking you been have.
8. I to haven't anything had drink.

Stopped by the Police

I was driving home the other night when I heard a siren behind me. It was a police car following me. I felt nervous. I pulled over to the curb and rolled my window down but kept my hands on the steering wheel so the officer could see them. I said, "What's the problem, Officer?" He said, "Show me your driver's license and your registration, please." I said, "Here they are," and took them out of my wallet to show him. He said, "Where are you going? Have you been drinking?" I said I was going home and hadn't had anything to drink. The police officer gave me back my license and registration and said, "Okay, sorry to bother you. Drive safely now." I felt much better and drove home.

Questions:

1. What do we do when we are driving and hear a siren behind us?
2. What other sirens might we hear besides a police siren?
3. Is it okay to give the officer money?
4. Why should the driver keep his hands up on the steering wheel?
5. Why is it best to be polite and cooperative when stopped by police?

Listening Cloze: Nouns

I was driving _____ the other _____ when I heard a _____ behind me. It was a police _____ following me. I felt nervous. I pulled over to the _____ and rolled my _____ down but kept my _____ on the steering _____ so the _____ could see them. I said, "What's the _____, Officer?" He said, "Show me your driver's _____ and your _____, please." I said, "Here they are," and took them out of my _____ to show him. He said, "Where are you going? Have you been drinking?" I said I was going _____ and hadn't had anything to drink. The police _____ gave me back my _____ and _____ and said, "Okay, sorry to bother you. Drive safely now." I felt much better and drove _____.

Listening Cloze: Verbs

I _____ driving home the other night when I _____ a siren behind me. It _____ a police car _____ me. I _____ nervous. I _____ over to the curb and _____ my window down but _____ my hands on the steering wheel so the officer _____ _____ them. I _____, "What's the problem, Officer?" He said, "_____ me your driver's license and your registration, please." I said, "Here they _____," and _____ them out of my wallet to _____ him. He said, "Where _____ you _____? _____ you _____ _____?" I said I _____ _____ home and _____n't _____ anything to _____. The police officer _____ me back my license and registration and said, "Okay, sorry to _____ you. _____ safely now." I_____ much better and _____ home.

UNIT 4: Buying a Used Car (Picture Story)

UNIT 4: Buying a Used Car (Key Words)

Bank account	Look online
Talk to people	Phone
Transfer	Test-drive
Mechanic	Postdated check

UNIT 4: Buying a Used Car (Sentences)

Check your
bank account.

Look at newspapers, at
magazines, and online.

Talk to people
who have bought
used cars.

Find the car you want
and phone to see it.

Go with the seller
to transfer the registration.

Bring a smart friend and
test-drive the car.

Take it to a mechanic
for a checkup.

Buy the car using a check that
you postdate a few days.

UNIT 4: Buying a Used Car (Reading and Listening)

1. Check your bank account.
2. Talk to people who have bought used cars.
3. Look at newspapers, at magazines, and online.
4. Find the car you want and phone to see it.
5. Bring a smart friend and test-drive the car.
6. Take it to a mechanic for a checkup.
7. Go with the seller to transfer the registration.
8. Buy the car using a check that you postdate a few days.

Scrambled Words

1. back canunot
2. thugbo
3. refsnart
4. canhimenc

5. zigsamnea
6. henop
7. eqhuce
8. drefin

Scrambled Sentences

1. friend test bring and car a the smart drive.
2. postdated the car using a buy check.
3. account your bank check.
4. online and look newspapers at magazines.
5. with the transfer go the registration to seller.
6. phone the car to see it and want you find.
7. used people have bought to who talk cars.
8. test the car a bring friend and smart drive.

How to Buy a Used Car

You might want a new car, but a used car that is only a few years old and in good condition is a much better bargain. Check your bank account to see what you can afford. Look at newspapers, magazines, and check online. When you find a car you want, take a smart friend with you and go see it. Take it for a test-drive. Take it to a mechanic and ask him to check it over. Spending $100 now is better than spending $1,000 later. If you decide to buy it, don't pay cash. Pay with a check that takes a few days to process. Then go with the owner to the Motor Vehicle branch to transfer the registration. If the car is okay, you have done well. If the car falls apart the next day, stop your check and take the car back to the original owner.

Questions:

1. Why buy a used car instead of a new car?
2. What should you do on a test-drive?
3. Which make of car do you prefer?
4. What does "good gas mileage" mean?
5. What is a hybrid car?
6. What does "winterize" your car mean?
7. What do you do before you take your car through a car wash?
8. How do you change a tire?
9. What are the rules about babies traveling in cars?
10. What do you think is safer—buying a used car from a well-known dealer or buying from someone you don't know?

Listening Cloze: Verbs

You might _____ a new car, but a used car that _____ only a few years old and in good condition _____ a much better bargain. _____ your bank account to _____ what you _____ afford. _____ at newspapers, magazines, and _____ online. When you _____ a car you want, _____ a smart friend with you and _____ _____ it. _____ it for a test-drive. _____ it to a mechanic and _____ him to _____ it over. Spending $100 now _____ better than spending $1,000 later. If you _____ to _____ it, _____n't _____ cash. _____ with a check that _____ a few days to process. Then _____ with the owner to the Motor Vehicle branch to _____ the registration. If the car _____ okay, you _____ _____ well.

If the car _____ apart the next day, _____ your check and _____ the car back to the original owner.

Listening Cloze: Articles and Prepositions

You might want _____ new car, but _____ used car that is only a _____ years old and _____ good condition is _____ much better bargain. Check your bank account _____ see what you can afford. Look _____ newspapers, magazines, and check online. When you find _____ car you want, take _____ smart friend _____ you and go see it. Take it _____ _____ test-drive. Take it _____ _____ mechanic and ask him _____ check it over. Spending $100 now is better than spending $1,000 later. If you decide _____ buy it, don't pay cash. Pay _____ _____ check that takes _____ few days _____ process. Then go _____ _____ owner _____ _____ Motor Vehicle branch _____ transfer _____ registration. If _____ car is okay, you have done well. If _____ car falls apart _____ next day, stop your check and take _____ car back _____ _____ original owner.

UNIT 5: Grocery Shopping (Picture Story)

UNIT 5: Grocery Shopping (Key Words)

Take a cart	Go grocery shopping
Pay the bill	Line up
Go up and down	Put them on the moving belt
Make a list	Go around

UNIT 5: Grocery Shopping (Sentences)

Put a quarter or a loonie in the slot and take a grocery cart.

Pay the bill with cash, check, or credit card.

Go up and down the inner aisles for snacks, treats, soft drinks, canned foods, juice, and frozen foods.

Check your kitchen, plan your meals, and make a list of things that you need.

Go to the supermarket.

Line up at the checkout counter.

Put your groceries on the moving belt.

Go around the outside aisles for perishable foods like vegetables, fruits, meat, fish, dairy, and baked goods.

UNIT 5: Grocery Shopping (Reading and Listening)

1. Check your kitchen, plan your meals, and make a list of things you need.
2. Go to the supermarket.
3. Put a coin in the slot and take a grocery cart.
4. Go up and down the inner aisles for items that last a long time.
5. Go around the outside aisles for items that do not last a long time.
6. Line up at the checkout counter.
7. Put your groceries on the moving belt.
8. Pay the bill.

Scrambled Words

1. yercor ract
2. slesia nenir
3. ketram repus
4. resiecorg
5. darc tiderc
6. netichk
7. tablesegev
8. touchkec

Scrambled Sentences

1. in a quarter the slot put.
2. for the go around outside vegetables.
3. pay cash bill with the.
4. the groceries moving your belt on put.
5. the drinks go down for aisles inner soft.
6. the supermarket to go.
7. make a plan and list your shopping meals.
8. out line at the check up.

Grocery Shopping

Before going grocery shopping, make a shopping list. Eat something so you don't go shopping when you're hungry. Go to the supermarket. If you have your own cloth bags, remember to take them. Put a coin into the slot and take a shopping cart. Go up and down the center aisles to buy the nonperishables, the items that keep a long time. Then go around the outside aisle to get foods that are perishable, those that will not keep. Buy ice cream last. Then go to the checkout counter and put your items on the moving belt. Present any coupons or reward cards to the clerk. If you've brought your own bags, give them to the clerk. Place the filled bags in your shopping cart. Pay with cash or credit card. Take your groceries and return the cart to get your coin back.

Questions:

1. Why buy ice cream last?
2. Why is it a good idea to make a shopping list first?
3. How can you tell if vegetables and fruits are fresh?
4. What is the different between skim milk and 3 percent?
5. Why do people open up egg cartons and look inside?
6. What is a "green grocer"?
7. What is a "butcher"?
8. Why do stores put candy bars and magazines at the checkout counter?
9. Why do people bring their own cloth bags to the supermarket?
10. What is the "sell by" date?

Listening Cloze: Nouns

Before going _____ shopping, make a shopping _____. Eat something so you don't go shopping when you're hungry. Go to the _____. If you have your own cloth _____, remember to take them. Put a _____ into the _____ and take a shopping _____. Go up and down the center _____ to buy the nonperishables, the items that keep a long time. Then go around the outside aisle to get _____ that are perishable, those that will not keep. Buy _____ last. Then go to the checkout _____ and put your _____ on the moving _____. Present any _____ or reward _____ to the _____. If you've brought your own _____, give them to the _____. Place the filled _____ in your shopping _____. Pay with _____ or credit _____. Take your _____ and return the _____ to get your _____ back.

Listening Cloze: Verbs

Before _____ grocery shopping, _____ a shopping list. _____ something so you _____n't _____ _____ when you're hungry. _____ to the supermarket. If you _____ your own cloth bags, _____ to take them. _____ a coin into the slot and _____ a shopping cart. _____ up and down the center aisles to _____ the nonperishables, the items that _____ a long time. Then _____ around the outside aisle to _____ foods that _____ perishable, those that _____ not _____. _____ ice cream last. Then _____ to the checkout counter and _____ your items on the moving belt. _____ any coupons or reward cards to the clerk. If you'_____ _____ your own bags, _____ them to the clerk. _____ the filled bags in your shopping cart. _____ with cash or credit card. _____ your groceries and _____ the cart to _____ your coin back.

UNIT 6: Making Tea (Picture Story)

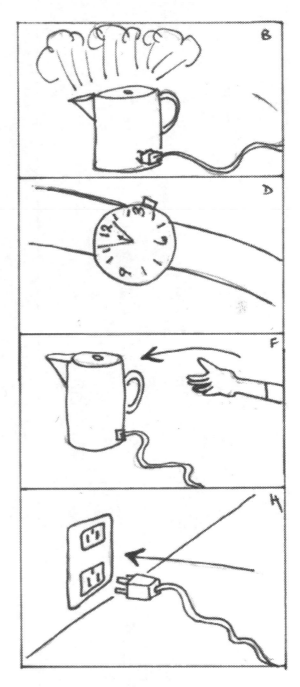

UNIT 6: Making Tea (Key Words)

Pour	Plug
Put	Boil
Fill	Get
Get	Wait

UNIT 6 Making Tea: Sentences

Put some tea in it.

Boil the water.

Get a teapot.

Wait one minute.

Pour the boiling water into the teapot.

Get a kettle.

Fill it with water.

Plug it in.

UNIT 6: Making Tea (Reading and Listening)

1. Get a kettle.
2. Fill it with water.
3. Plug it in.
4. Boil the water.
5. Get a teapot.
6. Put some tea in it.
7. Pour the boiling water into the teapot.
8. Wait one minute.

Scrambled Words

1. eat
2. rewet
3. pattoae
4. tinemua
5. ginilob
6. letket
7. if till
8. gulp

Scrambled Sentences

1. in plug it.
2. kettle a get.
3. water it with fill.
4. the teapot water into the pour boiling.
5. a get teapot.
6. water the boil.
7. some put in tea it.
8. minute one wait.

Making Tea

First, you get a kettle. Then you fill the kettle with water. You plug it in and boil the water. Next, you get a teapot and put some tea in it (one teaspoon for each person and one for the pot). Now you pour the boiling water into the teapot and wait one minute. Now get a cup and saucer and pour yourself a cup of tea. You can now add some sugar or some milk, or you can drink it plain.

After water, the most popular drink in the world is tea. It is said that tea was invented accidentally in China about 4,700 years ago when some leaves from a tea bush fell into a pot of boiling water. It came to Europe in the 1600s. Some people use loose tea, but most people use tea bags, which were invented by a coffee merchant, Thomas Sullivan. Today people drink tea made from dried leaves of many different plants.

Questions:

1. What is the most popular drink in the world?
2. What is the second most popular drink in the world?
3. What do you think is the third most popular drink?
4. What happens if the water for the tea is not boiling?
5. Which is the healthier drink for children— tea, coffee, milk, or juice?
6. Does all tea have caffeine in it?
7. Should you drink tea late in the evening? Why or why not?
8. Why do tea cups turn brown inside?
9. When did Europeans start drinking tea?
10. When did the Chinese and Japanese start drinking tea?

Listening Cloze: Nouns

First, you get a _____. Then you fill the _____ with _____. You plug it in and boil the _____. Next, you get a _____ and put some _____ in it (one _____ for each _____ and one for the _____). Now you pour the boiling _____ into the _____ and wait one _____. Now get a _____ and _____ and pour yourself a _____ of _____. You can now add some _____ or some _____, or you can drink it plain.

Listening Cloze: Verbs

After water, the most popular drink in the world _____ tea. It _____ _____ that tea _____ _____ accidentally in China about 4,700 years ago when some leaves from a tea bush _____ into a pot of boiling water. It _____ to Europe in the 1600s. Some people _____ loose tea, but most people _____ tea bags, which _____ _____ by a coffee merchant, Thomas Sullivan. Today people _____ tea made from dried leaves of many different plants.

UNIT 7: Cooking a Turkey (Picture Story)

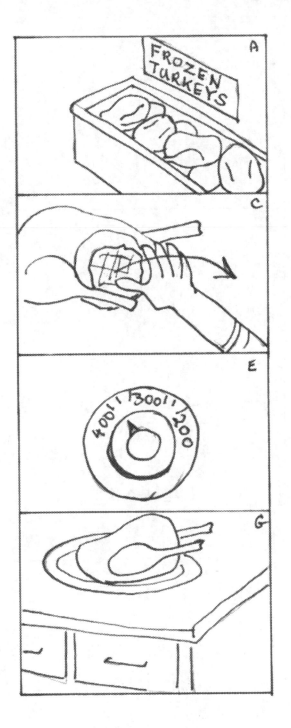

UNIT 7: Cooking a Turkey (Key Words)

Buy	Make
Take out	Roast
Preheat	Defrost
Let it rest	Put it in

UNIT 7: Cooking a Turkey (Sentences)

Buy a frozen turkey.

Stuff the turkey.

Take out the insides.

Roast it until it's golden brown.

Preheat the oven to 350 degrees.

Defrost it.

Take it out and let it rest fifteen minutes before carving.

Put the turkey in a roasting pan in the oven.

UNIT 7: Cooking a Turkey (Reading and Listening)

1. Buy a frozen turkey.
2. Defrost it.
3. Take out the insides.
4. Preheat the oven to 350 degrees.
5. Stuff the turkey.
6. Put the turkey in a roasting pan in the oven.
7. Roast it until it's golden brown.
8. Take it out and let it rest fifteen minutes before carving.

Scrambled Words

1. yekret
2. grown bolden
3. norzef
4. issidens

5. therape
6. ringvac
7. storefd
8. torasing

Scrambled Sentences

1. carving rest before fifteen minutes let it.
2. turkey the stuffing inside the put.
3. the 350 preheat degrees to oven.
4. the out insides take.
5. in a pan put the roasting oven turkey in the.
6. a turkey buy frozen.
7. defrost the turkey in the fridge over night.
8. in the night defrost the in fridge the turkey.

Cooking a Turkey

First, buy a frozen turkey big enough to feed everyone. Then take it home and defrost it by letting it sit unwrapped, covered lightly, in the fridge overnight. Then wash it and remove any of the organs left in it. Preheat the oven to 350 degrees.

Make some stuffing with bread crumbs or rice, chopped or ground cooked meat, onion, dried fruits and herbs of choice. Stuff the large body cavity and the small neck cavity. Tie the wings down and sew the neck cavity. Pull the tail flap over the drumsticks to close the body cavity. Put the turkey on a rack in a large roasting pan and put it in the oven.

If you cover it with a lid or aluminum foil, you don't have to baste it. If it is not covered, baste it every twenty minutes. Roast the turkey twenty minutes per pound or forty minutes per kilogram. When it is golden brown, and the leg can be moved easily, take it out of the oven. Let it rest for at least 15 minutes. Carve the turkey and set the slices of meat, the wings and the legs, on a large platter for the table.

Questions:

1. Is a turkey a big chicken?
2. Why don't you use a higher temperature to cook the turkey?
3. What can you do if your turkey is bigger than your pan?
4. What if you need to defrost your turkey quickly?
5. What is usually served with a roast turkey?

Listening Cloze: Verbs

First, _____ a frozen turkey big enough to _____ everyone. Then _____ it home and _____ it by letting it _____ unwrapped, covered lightly, in the fridge overnight. Then _____ it and _____ any of the organs left in it. _____ the oven to 350 degrees.

_____ some stuffing with bread crumbs or rice, chopped or ground cooked meat, onion, dried fruits and herbs of choice. S_____ the large body cavity and the small neck cavity. _____ the wings down and _____ the neck cavity. _____ the tail flap over the drumsticks to _____ the body cavity. _____ the turkey on a rack in a large roasting pan and _____ it in the oven.

If you _____ it with a lid or aluminum foil, you _____n't _____ to baste it. If it _____ not _____, _____ it every twenty minutes. _____ the turkey twenty minutes per pound or forty minutes per kilogram. When it _____ golden brown, and the leg _____ be _____ easily, _____ it out of the oven. L_____ it rest _____ at least fifteen minutes. _____ the turkey and _____ the slices of meat, the wings and the legs, on a large platter for the table.

UNIT 8: A Christmas Tree (Picture Story)

UNIT 8: A Christmas Tree (Key Words)

Put ornaments	Buy
Put on	Buy lights
Electrical outlet	A tree stand
Put an angel	Take

UNIT 8: A Christmas Tree (Sentences)

Buy a Christmas tree.

Buy lights and ornaments.

Buy a tree stand.

Put the tree in its stand.

Put an angel or star
on the top of the tree.

Take the tree home.

Put on the lights.

Put ornaments on the tree

UNIT 8: A Christmas Tree (Reading and Listening)

1. Buy a Christmas tree.
2. Buy a tree stand.
3. Buy lights and ornaments, garlands or streamers, and a star or an angel for the top.
4. Take the tree home.
5. Put the tree in its stand.
6. Put the lights on the tree.
7. Put the ornaments on the tree and wrap the garlands or streamers around the tree.
8. Put the angel or the star at the top of the tree.

Scrambled Words

1. stmenanor
2. legan
3. stighl
4. samtrichs
5. rats
6. eter
7. ybu a dants
8. ehmo

Scrambled Sentences

1. the home tree take.
2. lights on put the.
3. ornaments the tree on put.
4. on the star put the tree or an angel top of.
5. tree a christmas buy.
6. stand a buy tree.
7. put its stand in the tree.
8. lights buy ornaments and.

A Christmas Tree

First, decide whether you want a real Christmas tree or an artificial one. Then go out and buy a tree that will fit in your living room. Buy a tree stand and special tree lights. Buy or make ornaments and a star or an angel for the top. The colors are usually red, green, white, blue, gold, and silver. We do not usually use pink or orange colors at Christmas. When you get home, put the tree in a stand near an electrical outlet but not near a fireplace or a heat radiator. If the tree is artificial and needs to be assembled, be sure to arrange the large branches at the bottom and the small branches at the top. If the tree is real, arrange a container so that you can keep the tree watered. Now put the tree lights on the tree. Wind the lights around the tree and put the star or angel at the top. Put on the ornaments and then wind the garlands or streamers around the tree. Now plug in the lights and check to see that everything is spaced evenly all over the tree. Place wrapped Christmas presents under the tree.

Questions:

1. Why do people choose artificial trees?
2. Why do you have to water a real tree?
3. Why do we put the largest branches at the bottom?
4. Why do people have only evergreen trees for Christmas trees?
5. Why do people have lots of lights and candles at Christmas?

Listening Cloze: Nouns

First, decide whether you want a real Christmas _____ or an artificial _____. Then go out and buy a _____ that will fit in your living _____. Buy a tree _____ and special tree _____. Buy or make _____ and a _____ or an _____ for the top. The _____ are usually red, _____, white, _____, gold, and _____. We do not usually use pink or orange _____ at _____. When you get _____, put the _____ in a _____ near an electrical _____ but not near a _____ or a heat _____. If the _____ is artificial and needs to be assembled, be sure to arrange the large _____ at the _____ and the small _____ at the top. If the _____ is real, arrange a _____ so that you can keep the _____ watered. Now put the tree _____ on the _____. Wind the _____ around the tree and put the _____ or _____ at the _____. Put on the _____, and then wind the _____ or streamers around the tree. Now plug in the _____ and check to see that everything is spaced evenly all over the tree. Place wrapped Christmas _____ under the _____.

UNIT 9: Silent Night (Picture Story)

UNIT 9: Silent Night (Key Words)

Christmas Eve	Worked all night.
Will you please . . . ?	Big problem!
Everyone singing.	Ran fast
Nearly Christmas	Doesn't work.

UNIT 9: Silent Night (Sentences)

The organ was broken.

It was nearly Christmas.

The priest didn't know
what to do.

He played and sang
the new song.
All the people
joined in the joyful singing.

He ran to the church
as fast as he could.
He got there just as
the Christmas Eve service
was starting.

It was Christmas Eve, and all the
people were expecting a beautiful
church service with lovely music.

He worked all night and
all day until at last the
new song was finished.

The church organist agreed
to try to write a simple song
to be sang with a guitar.

UNIT 9: Silent Night (Reading and Listening)

1. It was nearly Christmas.
2. The organ was broken.
3. The priest didn't know what to do.
4. The church organist agreed to try to write a simple song to be sang with a guitar.
5. He worked all night and all day until at last the new song was finished.
6. It was Christmas Eve.
7. He ran to the church as fast as he could and got there just as the service was starting.
8. He played and sang the new song, and all the people joined in the joyful singing.

Scrambled Words

1. sitmarchs
2. nebork
3. ratiug
4. curhch

5. opplee
6. gginnis
7. sumic
8. lemborp

Scrambled Sentences

1. song sung simple write a guitar to be with.
2. what to do didn't priest the know.
3. christmas nearly was it.
4. was organ the broken.
5. he and played sang song new the.
6. eve was Christmas it.
7. church ran to the he as he could fast.
8. was at song last the finished.

The Story of Silent Night

Just before Christmas in 1818, at St. Nicholas' Church at Obendorf Village in the snow-covered mountains near Salzburg, Austria, there was a serious problem. The church organ was broken. All they had for music at the important Christmas Eve service was the guitar. They needed something very special to make Christmas Eve perfect. The organist, Franz Gruber, was asked to write guitar music for a simple poem, which the priest's assistant, Joseph Mohr, had written, so the people would have a special new song for their special night. The organist agreed and worked night and day on the new song. Finally, just before the Christmas Eve service began, he finished the song and ran as fast as he could to the church. The music was shared out, and Franz Gruber played the new song on the guitar. The people of Obendorf had a beautiful new Christmas carol. The hymn "Silent Night" was born. Now people all over the world sing "Silent Night" by Joseph Mohr and Franz Gruber on Christmas Eve.

Questions:

1. Name the village where "Silent Night" was first sung.
2. Who wrote the music to "Silent Night"?
3. What is a Christmas carol?
4. What is an organ, and what is a guitar?
5. In what season of the year in North America does Christmas come?
6. In Australia, in what season is Christmas?
7. Name three other Christmas songs?
8. What's another way of saying "Father Christmas" or "Pere Noel"?
9. What's the ninth reindeer's name?
10. Why are Christmas trees always evergreen trees?

Listening Cloze: Verbs

Just before Christmas in 1818, at St. Nicholas' Church at Obendorf Village in the snow-covered mountains near Salzburg, Austria, there _____ a serious problem. The church organ _____ broken. All they _____ for music at the important Christmas Eve service _____ the guitar. They _____ something very special to _____ Christmas Eve perfect. The organist, Franz Gruber, _____ _____ to _____ guitar music for a simple poem, which the priest's assistant, Joseph Mohr, _____ _____, so the people _____ _____ a special new song for their special night. The organist _____ and worked night and day on the new song. Finally, just before the Christmas Eve service began, he _____ the song and _____ as fast as he could to the church. The music _____ _____ out, and Franz Gruber _____ the new song on the guitar. The people of Obendorf _____ a beautiful new Christmas carol. The hymn "Silent Night" _____ _____. Now people all over the world _____ "Silent Night" by Joseph Mohr and Franz Gruber on Christmas Eve.

Listening Cloze: Nouns

Just before _____ in 1818, at St. Nicholas' _____ at Obendorf _____ in the snow-covered _____ near _____, _____, there was a serious _____. The church _____ was broken. All they had for _____ at the important Christmas Eve _____ was the _____. They needed something very special to make Christmas _____ perfect. The organist, _____ _____, was asked to write guitar _____ for a simple _____, which the priest's _____, Joseph Mohr, had written so the _____ would have a special new _____ for their special _____. The _____ agreed and worked _____ and _____ on the new _____. Finally, just before the Christmas Eve _____ began, he finished the _____ and ran as fast as he could to the _____. The _____ was shared out, and Franz Gruber played the new _____ on the _____. The _____ of _____ had a beautiful new Christmas _____. The _____ "Silent _____" was born. Now _____ all over the _____ sing "Silent Night" by Joseph Mohr and Franz Gruber on Christmas _____.

UNIT 10: The Burglar (Picture Story)

UNIT 10: The Burglar (Key Words)

This way, that way.	Heard
Call 911	Stop!
Sleep	Got him!
What happened?	Noise.

UNIT 10: The Burglar (Sentences)

You go that way,
I'll go this way.

I heard it too.

Call 911!
We've caught a burglar.

Hey! You! Stop!

I don't hear anything.
Let me sleep.

I've got him!

What happened?

I heard a noise.

UNIT 10: The Burglar (Reading and Listening)

1. I heard a noise.
2. I heard it too.
3. I don't hear anything. Let me sleep.
4. You go that way, I'll go this way.
5. Hey! You! Stop!
6. I've got him.
7. Call 911! We caught a burglar.
8. What happened?

Scrambled Words

1. senio
2. dearh
3. larbrug
4. elsep
5. Yeh! Pots!
6. hath yaw
7. thaguc
8. pendaphe

Scrambled Sentences

1. hear did that you.
2. back sleep he to went.
3. into hall they the crept.
4. front go I'll up stairs the.
5. got umbrella an Shirley.
6. officer the neighbor a was retired police.
7. quickly the came police very.
8. a caught burglar we've.

The Burglar

One night, about 2:00 a.m., Shirley was awakened by the sound of someone rattling her apartment door. Her mother came out of her bedroom and whispered, "Did you hear that too?" Then they peeked out into the hallway and saw a burglar going along the hall, trying each apartment door. They woke up Shirley's dad and whispered urgently, "Dad, wake up. There's a burglar." He answered, "Don't be ridiculous," and went back to sleep. Then Shirley got an umbrella, and her mother got a rolling pin, and they crept into the hall, but the burglar had already gone upstairs. Just then, the neighbor, a retired police officer, came out and said quietly, "Did you hear that?" Shirley said, "Yes, it's a burglar!" The neighbor said, "You two go up the back stairs, and I'll go up the front stairs, and we'll catch him." It worked!

A few minutes later, Shirley's dad came out and said sleepily, "What's happened?" Just then, the neighbor appeared, pushing the burglar and holding his arm behind his back. Shirley called 911 and said, "We've caught a burglar!" Her father was shocked and amazed! The police came very quickly. They searched the burglar and found work gloves and tools. The police were pleased. They knew the burglar well and were very pleased he was caught. They took him to jail. Everybody said good night and went back to bed.

Question:

1. What mistake did Shirley and her mother make?
2. What mistake did Shirley's dad make?
3. What mistake did the burglar make?
4. How long did they wait for the police to come?
5. Where did everyone go when it was all over?

Listening Cloze: Nouns

One _____, about 2:00 a.m., _____ was awakened by the _____ of someone rattling her apartment _____. Her mother came out of her _____ and whispered, "Did you hear that too?" Then they peeked out into the _____ and saw a _____ going along the _____, trying each apartment door. They woke up Shirley's _____ and whispered urgently, "Dad, wake up. There's a burglar." He answered, "Don't be ridiculous," and went back to _____. Then Shirley got an _____, and her _____ got a rolling _____, and they crept into the _____, but the burglar had already gone _____. Just then, the _____, a retired police _____, came out and said quietly, "Did you hear that?" Shirley said, "Yes, it's a _____!" The neighbor said, "You _____ go up the back _____, and I'll go up the front _____, and we'll catch him." It worked!

A few _____ later, Shirley's dad came out and said sleepily, "What's happened?" Just then, the _____ appeared, pushing the _____ and holding his _____ behind his _____. Shirley called 911 and said, "We've caught a _____!" Her _____ was shocked and amazed! The _____ came very quickly. They searched the burglar and found work _____ and _____. The police were pleased. They knew the burglar well and were very pleased he was caught. They took him to _____. Everybody said good _____ and went back to _____.

Unit 11: The Noisy Neighbor (Picture Story)

Unit 11: The Noisy Neighbor (Key Words)

Went to sleep.	Knocked at the door.
Felt sorry.	Felt angry.
Was vacuuming.	No problem.
Covered his ears.	Hello, friend and neighbor.

Unit 11: The Noisy Neighbor (Sentences)

Joe was a single young man
living in an apartment.
It was 11:00 p.m.,
so he went to bed
and closed his eyes.

She said she was cleaning her
apartment. She did not see
that it was past 11:00 p.m. She
said she wouldn't make any
more noise after 11:00 p.m.

He wanted to bang on the
ceiling and shout,
"Be quiet!"
But he knew getting angry
would not help him sleep.

Joe was very happy to have
met Lena, and he was really
happy that he did not get
angry about the noise.

So he went upstairs.
He knocked on the door.
A lovely young lady answered.
Joe introduced himself
and explained his problem.

Lena said she was
really happy to meet Joe.

The young lady said her name
was Lena. She was very pleased
to meet Joe, and she was
very sorry about the noise.

Suddenly, loud noises came from
the apartment above him. Joe
tried putting fingers in his ears. Nothing
helped. The noise just got louder.

Unit 11: The Noisy Neighbor (Reading and Listening)

1. Joe was a single young man living in an apartment. It was 11:00 p.m., so he went to bed and closed his eyes.
2. Suddenly, loud noises came from the apartment above him. Joe tried putting fingers in his ears. Nothing helped. The noise just got louder.
3. He wanted to bang on the ceiling and shout, "Be quiet!" But he knew getting angry would not help him sleep.
4. So he went upstairs. He knocked on the door. A lovely young lady answered. Joe introduced himself and explained his problem.
5. The young lady said her name was Lena. She was very pleased to meet Joe, and she was very sorry about the noise.
6. She said she was cleaning her apartment. She did not see that it was past 11:00 p.m. She said she wouldn't make any more noise after 11:00 p.m.
7. Lena said she was really happy to meet Joe.
8. Joe was very happy to have met Lena, and he was really happy that he did not get angry about the noise.

Scrambled Words

1. glesin
2. ttmenpara
3. sonie
4. tueqi
5. roblemp
6. rosyr
7. robgineh
8. issairput
9. cumavu
10. morbo

Scrambled Sentences

1. bed to he went and sleep he went sleep to.
2. him above noises came loud apartment from the.
3. ceiling bang wanted to he the on.
4. answered lady a lovely young.
5. the noise was she sorry about very.

Unit 11: The Noisy Neighbor

Joe was a single young man living alone in an apartment. One night, at eleven o'clock, he felt tired, and so he went to bed, closed his eyes, and went to sleep. Suddenly, loud noises came from the apartment above him. Joe tried putting his pillow over his head and putting his fingers in his ears. Nothing helped. The noise just got louder and louder! He wanted to bang on the ceiling with a broom and shout, "Be quiet!" But he knew getting angry would just make him wide awake. So he put on his slippers and robe and went upstairs. He knocked on the door. He was surprised when a lovely young lady answered. Joe introduced himself and explained his problem, trying not to sound too angry. The young lady said her name was Lena, she was very pleased to meet Joe, and she was very sorry about the noise. She said she was cleaning her apartment, and she did not notice that it was so late. She said she wouldn't make noise after 11:00 p.m. ever again. Lena also said she was really happy to meet her neighbor, Joe. Joe was also very happy to have met Lena, and he was really happy that he did not get angry about the noise. His neighbor was now his girlfriend.

Questions

1. Was Joe married?
2. Where did the noise come from?
3. What did he feel like doing?
4. What did Joe actually do?
5. Who was upstairs?
6. What is an apology?

Sandra Price-Hosie

Unit 11: The Noisy Neighbor Listening Cloze

Joe was a single young _____ living alone in an _____. It was 11:00 p.m., so he went to bed, closed his _____, and went to sleep. Suddenly, loud _____ came from the apartment _____ him. Joe tried putting his pillow over his _____ and putting his fingers in his _____. Nothing helped. The noise just got _____. He wanted to bang on the ceiling with a _____ and shout, "Be quiet!" But he knew getting _____ would not help him sleep.

UNIT 12: My Story (Pictures)

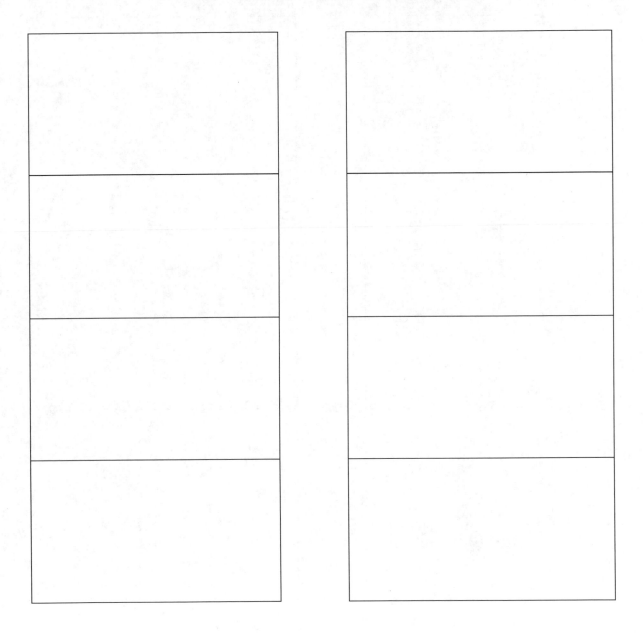

Unit 12: My Story (Key Words)

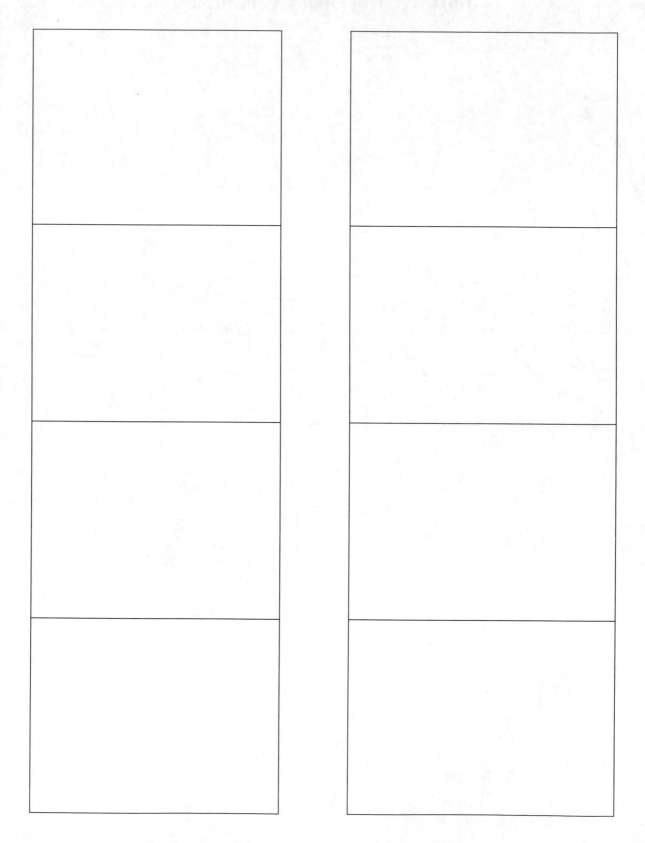

Unit 12: My Story (Sentences)

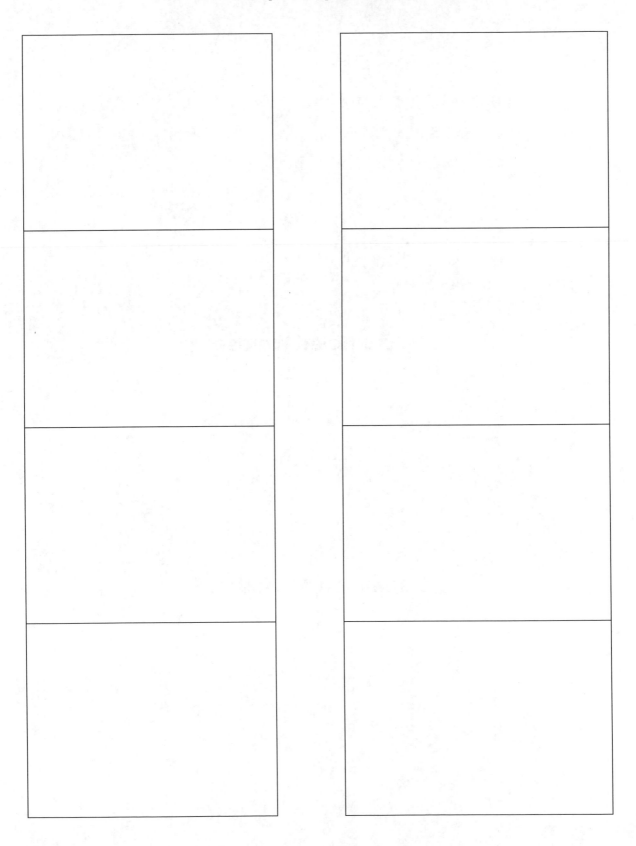

Unit 12: Sentences in Correct Order

Scrambled Words

Scrambled Sentences

My Story

Questions

Listening Cloze

The End.

Printed in the United States
By Bookmasters